# LADYBUGS

## INSECTS

James P. Rowan

The Rourke Corporation, Inc.
Vero Beach, Florida 32964

Edited by Sandra A. Robinson

PHOTO CREDITS
© Lynn M. Stone: cover, title page, page 18; © James P. Rowan:
pages 4, 8, 10, 12; © Frank Balthis: pages 7, 13, 17, 21; © Jerry
Hennen: page 15

**Library of Congress Cataloging-in-Publication Data**

Rowan, James P.
    Ladybugs / by James P. Rowan.
        p.   cm. — (The Insect discovery library)
    Includes index.
    Summary: An introduction to the physical characteristics, habits,
and behavior of ladybugs.
    ISBN 0-86593-291-3
    1. Ladybirds—Juvenile literature. [1. Ladybugs.] I. Title.
 II. Series.
QL596.C65R69   1993
595.76'9—dc20                                    89-32921
                                                      CIP
Printed in the USA                                    AC

# TABLE OF CONTENTS

Ladybugs                          5
Kinds of Ladybugs                 6
What Ladybugs Eat                 9
New Ladybugs                      11
Where Ladybugs Live               14
Ladybug Enemies                   16
Hibernation                       19
Ladybugs from Other Lands         20
Ladybugs and People               22
Glossary                          23
Index                             24

# LADYBUGS

Ladybugs belong to the group of insects known as beetles. Beetles have a hard pair of **forewings** that rest over their backs. The forewings protect the delicate **hindwings** that are folded underneath.

Most ladybugs are round and less than 1/2 inch long. Many are orange or red with black spots on the forewings. Some are black with yellow or red spots.

Since ladybugs are really beetles, they are sometimes called lady beetles.

*The typical ladybug, or lady beetle, is orange with black spots*

## KINDS OF LADYBUGS

There are over 400 **species,** or kinds, of ladybugs in North America. Some are named for the markings on their forewings. The two-spotted, nine-spotted, and fifteen-spotted ladybugs were named this way. So were the striped, three-banded and **parenthesis** ladybugs.

Another ladybug, the mealybug destroyer, earned its name by eating so many mealybugs. The red mite destroyer was named for its appetite, too.

*Many ladybugs are named for the number of black spots on their backs*

## WHAT LADYBUGS EAT

Most ladybugs eat other kinds of insects. Aphids, mealybugs, scale insects and mites are favorite foods of many ladybug species. Because ladybugs hunt and feed on other animals, they are called **predators**.

A few kinds of ladybugs are not predators, however. The Mexican bean beetle and the squash beetle feed on plants. They can be serious pests for these crops. They are the "black sheep"—the troublemakers—of the ladybug family.

*The spotless ladybug dines on its favorite prey, an aphid*

# NEW LADYBUGS

The life cycle of a ladybug has four stages—the egg, larva, pupa and adult. The female ladybug usually lays her eggs near a group of aphids or mealybugs. When the ladybug egg hatches, the larva feeds on the nearby insects.

The larva feeds for several months. It then becomes inactive—it doesn't eat or move—in the third, or pupa, stage. During the pupa stage, the larva becomes an adult ladybug.

*A ladybug larva feeds on other insects before becoming a pupa*

11

*Ladybug pupa is an inactive stage in the insect's life*

*Ladybugs gather on a fallen tree in California*

# WHERE LADYBUGS LIVE

Ladybugs live wherever they can find **prey,** or food. Since aphids and mealybugs feed on plants, that's where ladybugs are.

Usually ladybugs live in open fields, grasslands, forests and yards. The Mexican bean beetle and squash beetle live on farms where beans and squash are grown. When they are not feeding, ladybugs sometimes hide in flowers or beneath leaves.

*Ladybugs visit plants where their prey lives*

# LADYBUG ENEMIES

Ladybugs are eaten by most animals that feed on insects. A jumping spider may leap upon a ladybug that is looking for aphids. A **praying mantis** may grab a ladybug off a leaf.

A ladybug might fly into the sticky web of a garden spider and be eaten. A bird may catch one in mid-air.

Some kinds of ladybugs, however, taste bad. Animals that have eaten these ladybugs probably do not want to catch ladybugs again.

16 *Ladybugs, shown crawling among madrone berries in California mountains, are often protected by their foul taste*

# HIBERNATION

Most species of ladybugs live only until the first frost of winter. However, some species **hibernate** or "sleep" through winter under logs or bark.

Sometimes a ladybug will hibernate in a house. When it wakes up in the spring, it may appear on a window as it tries to go outdoors.

A few kinds of ladybugs hibernate in groups of several thousand. Sometimes these groups are collected and used by farmers to control insect pests.

*After hibernation, a ladybug snacks on a spring wildflower*

## LADYBUGS FROM OTHER LANDS

Sometimes an insect pest—one that no one wants around—is accidentally brought from one country to another. In its new home, it may have few enemies to eat it.

The cottony cushion scale insect from Australia destroyed **citrus** trees in California during the 1800s. The Vedalia ladybug was brought from Australia to California in 1888 to prey upon the cushion scale and save the citrus.

*Ladybugs were brought to California to prey upon citrus-eating insects*

## LADYBUGS AND PEOPLE

People like ladybugs because they are colorful, and they eat garden and crop pests.

Ladybugs destroy large numbers of aphids, mealybugs and scale insects. These pest insects feed on the juices of plants. Many of them feeding together can kill the plants.

Some people raise ladybugs to sell to farmers and gardeners. This is a natural way to control insect pests, so fewer insect-killing poisons and chemicals are put into the ground and air.

# Glossary

**citrus** (SIH truhs) — a specific group of trees that produce fruits such as oranges and grapefruits

**forewings** (FOR wings) — the two front wings of a four-winged insect

**hibernate** (hi bur NATE) — to enter a deep sleep during which certain animals survive winter

**hindwings** (HIND wings) — the two rear wings of a four-winged insect

**parenthesis** (par EN theh sis) — a specific curved mark () that looks like the parenthesis mark used in writing

**praying mantis** (PRAY ing MAN tiss) — a large, strong-jawed insect that feeds on other insects

**predator** (PRED uh tor) — an animal that kills other animals for food

**prey** (PRAY) — an animal that is hunted for food by another animal

**species** (SPEE sheez) — within a group of closely-related animals, such as ladybugs, one certain kind or type (*two-spotted* ladybug)

# INDEX

aphids  9, 11, 14, 16, 22
Australia  20
beetles  5
    Mexican bean  9, 14
    squash  9, 14
California  20
citrus  20
egg  11
farmers  19, 22
forewings  5
hibernation  19
hindwings  5
insects  5, 9
ladybugs
    fifteen-spotted  6
    nine-spotted  6
    parenthesis  6
    striped  6
    three-banded  6
    two-spotted  6

larva  11
mealybug destroyer  6
mealybugs  6, 9, 11, 14, 22
mites  9
pests  9, 19, 20, 22
praying mantis  16
predators  9
prey  14
pupa  11
red mite destroyer  6
scale insects  9, 20, 22
species  6
spider
    garden  16
    jumping  16
stages  11
taste  16